I Hope This Hurts

SYDNEY STAPLETON

ISBN: 978-1-961028-90-6

Contents

Close your eyes and
wait for your mind
to eclipse

I haven't been sleeping

These tears have been seeping

And steadily weakening

The thoughts that have been creepin' in

My wounds are still fresh

Can't lick 'em just yet

Trying to back away from the cliff

I'm one inch from death

Thrown onto this battlefield

Feeling put to the test

But I'll pull my knuckles down

And give it my best

At night I write

Keeps me from feeling alone

These words to me are like family

Weird to get it when you grown

Parents in the room watching TV

Under the same roof but it's like they don't see me

Blind to what's going on in my mind

It's a jungle in there

Sanity would be too hard to find

Trying to keep it low-key

Managing my mischief

In secrecy like Loki

Then here comes the thunder

Thanks a lot brother

Attempting to bury deep what you're so desperate to uncover

And to the mother I once had

And the sister she brought with her

I know it's a hard pill to swallow

But no need to be bitter

If it's words on a screen

Or written on a page

Doesn't really matter

Same shit, different day

Never had my dream right in front of me

It's like I'm at the end of the book

And still haven't figured out the mystery

To always have the focus on someone else and being rejected

It's like I'm trying to explain myself

But you still don't get it

Not a violent person, and your mold, I won't break it

It's like I'm designing my own

But you still try to reshape it

Constantly at a loss for something I should know well

It's like finally having that encouragement

And still can't propel

Working my brain 'til the last lobe is ready to combust

It's like I'm doing all that I can

Yet still, it's not enough

I'm just not feeling it

Only thing I'm feeling is the urge to quit

Being tested by all the things I've digested is making me sick

I swallowed them down

But they keep coming back up

Being stuck in the same rut is starting to suck

I need a change of scenery

But the grass on the other side doesn't look that green to me

Time has got me in a bind

The clock has officially stopped

Can't move forward or hit rewind

My motivation is inescapably blocked

My knight in rusted armor

He is so naïve

Talking all the time

I need to concentrate

Tuning him out

Sometimes hard to do

Feigning a smile

He is so naïve

A heart that had no soul

Beating coldly in a hollow chest

Touched by the warmth of love

A familiar feeling

But different in so many ways

The mind is no longer a prison of unwanted thoughts

But a haven to escape the cruelty of the world

With a body that is set on fire

Only two pools of the clearest blue can soothe

Everything is okay again

All she has to do is jump in

And my eyes just can't read fast enough

The map of your body is extraordinary

Though I'm not sure I like where this is going

You tell me things that sound wonderful

Yet I'm led around in circles

I walk along the crevices of your mind

But I'm lost in the confusion of all you say to me

If I could get a grip on your sides

Hold myself steady

The journey wouldn't seem so hard

My breathing wouldn't be so heavy

I could relax and enjoy the view

Though the trek hasn't been so easy

And the weather's been rough around the edges

It's something I needed to do

At least now I know I'm ready

Sleep deprived and I know why

Thoughts of you won't leave my mind

I toss and turn all night

My eyes are open wide

It's hot then it's cold

My body can't decide

I'm dealing with different shit

My heart's racing and it's losing quick

I know you notice when my hands shake

My cheeks turn red

And the many voices in my head

Fight over the things I should have said

I get no release to catch these zzz's

So I let my mind tire of you

And then in my dreams

There you are too

Prince, not so charming

I'm pretty sure I would rather be beaten half to death

Those wounds would heal a lot faster

Your words cut through me so violently

You spit them out as fast as a bullet leaves a gun

Sometimes I'm immune to the pain

I've heard it before anyway

But then you take it to a new hurtful level

One I'd hope to never reach

I'm not sure where to go from here

Or if we'll ever recover

You have my heart in one hand

And I'm dangling in the other

With each tear falling as you slowly let me sink further

Like any time before, I'm hoping you'll grasp my hand and pull me up

Letting what love you have for me banish the negativity

Keep my heart as a gift of my gratitude

Because I will never tire of loving you

He put his hands on me

Call me dumb, but I didn't see it coming

Slapped me across the face

Punched me in the chest

It's like he got off on it

Asked me if I knew what was coming next

To be honest, I didn't wanna be there to see the rest

Wish I could go back in time in my mind

Stay there for a while

Wouldn't have to deal with this

My situation wouldn't be so serious

I could live in denial

But I'm here not knowing what to do

Not knowing my next move

Or for that matter, his

No clue

And it's like this every day

He's got a hold on me that I'm struggling to break

Wondering if I'll ever stop the cycle

But his words just keep washing my brain

And they hurt worse than any amount of physical pain

Lately my wilting efforts have been falling just short of you noticing

It's like pulling teeth just to get on your not-too-mean side

I'm almost to the point where I've tried everything

Is this what it feels like when your heart dies?

I scream and nothing comes out

I hurt but there are no wounds

If you could just put your lips on my mouth

Tell me we'll be together soon

Go back to when you had a smile in your voice every time you talked to me

Made me feel like I was wanted by you and wouldn't need anyone else

Put your hand in mine and called me baby

Now it seems I'm all by myself

I know there is good in you because I've seen it before

I don't know when I'll see it but I hope that I do

Each day I fall in love with you more and more

Just say that you're in love with me too

My lover killed me again today

And again God sent me back

It is in anything he can think to say

That gives my heart another crack

So many that he just destroys me

Each time I tell God my heart can't take it

I love him and I try to believe

But his rage flame is already lit

God tells me this will take time

One day he will come around

Just as if I were in line

I wait patiently but am feeling so down

Another damaged brain

You're frustrating me and that's putting it nicely

No one else is gonna put up with this bullshit besides me

Every day got me feelin' low very highly

People really suck

They don't know not to try me

Trying to figure out why I'm still here is confusing

Steadily punching that clock until I see it bruising

Runnin' in a rat race that all of us are losing

Throw in my towel

This is not of my choosing

Waking up to the sound of waves and sun on my face

Couldn't ask for better days, never leaving this place

That's the kind of lifestyle I want to embrace

'Til then, I'm stuck here

Giving in to the chase

My life is a broken record

With emotions repeating the past

I think I've found myself

But couldn't be further from it

No, I don't aim to please

It's the last thing on my mind

What does it all mean?

That, I'm trying to find

I hate my sister

She won't leave me alone

She doesn't understand

This is no longer her home

She's become quite annoying

Her welcome overstayed

She doesn't get the hint

That my love is delayed

This food has no taste

And my stomach would agree

Though I cannot deny

The rumbling inside of me

I can see what is beneath

And it is a slight relief

But my body has grown weak

Since the bones have atrophied

The sun got darker

Outside is our sanctuary

We could drive travel-less or walk with no end in sight

The stars especially, oh so very

Climb high on mountains, stay hidden next to flight

Those two pools that call my name

Get stained red often, no matter the try

The blackest night couldn't cover the pain

Just stay with yours in mine until down it all dies

And when they come for your head and heart and soul

There is nothing wrong with you

It should be told that you were good

I could die tonight and be alright too

Didn't need any time alone

But that was what you gave me

I guess I can use it to my advantage

No choice but to take it

Yeah I'm gettin' smarter

My body is lookin' better

No one is coming my way

Must be the weather that is keeping them inside

My head is cloudy all the time

But when it starts to show

That's when I have nowhere to go

And the days move by real slow

So I keep to myself

And try not to stress

It's proving to be a challenge

Hard not to fret

When come to find out

You're just like the rest

Left me high and dry

Kinda lonely up here hangin'

And deafening listening to all the words you're not saying

But I'll use your absence to tap into my consciousness

Burn off my feelings like nerve endings

Take my brain to the gym

See if it sinks or swims

Cause there's a lot on my mind

Weighing me down

And I never knew it was there

Until I noticed you weren't around

You still haven't called

It makes my heart pound harder with every minute that passes

I can't stop thinking of yesterday

All the hurtful things you said

Trying not to think about it reminds me anyway

I'm more than willing to forget this ever happened

Let's just go back to how much I'm in love with you

In the end it doesn't matter what I would go through

So everything you would want in a person will just wait

While you waste all the time in the world

Using up all my feelings until I feel no more

Come and say that you love me, need me

And I'll just smile because you know you mean everything

I won't forget this feeling
It visits every now and then
The thought of you being with someone else brings me here
Taking my heart and leaving with her is what I fear

I only wanted to hurt you because you hurt me
But it backfired, and I know that's not the way to be
What I was trying to do was in a moment of weakness
This feeling was there too, when I was helpless

Realizing now I shouldn't have tried to let you go
Trying to explain how much I love you, would be too much to show
Sitting here with nothing but shame, guilt and hurt
I'm praying you will forgive me, and know this will work

My days painfully drag on and I'm mocked by time
This feeling has me reminiscing about when you were mine
I think about you now, and I don't know what to do
If I try to talk, I'll feel like I'm just bothering you

If I leave you be, it'll drive me insane
And there is no pill to take to relieve me of this pain
I can't imagine the thought that we could ever be over
That kind of thinking makes me not want to be sober

I can't handle that, can't let it be true

But if it is, this feeling will always be there

Holding me instead of you

Such a free soul, locked down

I'm uneducated

Got this fear in my mind that I'll never make it

Trying to get big wigs to notice me

They hate it

Contemplating these thoughts is frustrating

Starting and stopping

No progress in the making

It's cause they won't listen

Keeping me locked up in the talent prison

While they throw money at friends of friends of them

Producing crap

Wondering where the ambition went

It's all I can think about

They revel in my torment

Reflecting off the stained glass curtain

The scent of almonds projects from my pores

This is all fake as you are certain

My work is of nothing but me being bored

It is what it is, I will say again

It is what it is

Nothing more

Somehow it's like a dream

Not much is going on

But so much time has passed

At this point, I wake up

I'm aware that this is not a dream

Like sleeping with your eyes open

Everything is happening around me

And I see none of it

I relapsed

Fell back into my old habits

Like sweat drippin' down my face

Hard not to dab at it

But I hear this voice in my head

Tellin' me to grab at it

I need it in my life

The weakest excuse of a true addict

And funny when I have it

It doesn't make me feel better

It's just a fatal attraction

Leaving me forever tethered

You never think it can happen to you. I know that sounds cliché, but it's true

This is all just one big lie

You don't believe me

But I said I'd love you 'til the day you die

I never thought about it

Never would have cheated on you

But you were so convinced that false was true

This is the first time I have felt like this

So loved and wanted

So hated and dismissed

You broke my spirit

Took everything I had

Did anything to make you happy

But all you were was mad

I didn't care about your past

My future had us together

Apologized when I wasn't wrong

Trying to make things better

For whatever reason

You had this idea in your head

Made me out to be evil

Wanted our relationship dead

I proved you wrong

The evidence was all there

But you were singing the same old song

The same one for a year

I stuck around for love

Lived my life to your time

Nothing was ever good enough

Never mattered down the line

The ball was always in your court

You always had the upper hand

But I was just extra baggage

Another useless instrument in your band

You say I will move on

Find someone new

That's just the problem

There are no other yous

I am just a fool

Blind to the wrong you have caused me

That sickness in my stomach

This is what love must be

So what if I am dumb in love?

For you, inside me

I will vomit my heart as it beats

Watch it land at your feet

I am not a liar

Everything I've said is real

With my hand to God, I will shatter your paranoia

Do we have a deal?

It sickens me to do this

I guess there is no other way

My heart is in my throat, ready

I want you to stay

All I have to give

But it's still not enough

Under your cruel spell

Still giving you my love

Increasing your hate

Vacant of all feeling

Exhausting my wait

Never thought I'd be so weak

And let you take everything from me

My spirit is broken and my thoughts turned sour

I just keep asking myself, "how come?"

How come you're so mean all of a sudden?

You used to treat me better than anyone

Talk to me like I'm trash and look at me with hate

Murder me with your coldness and walk away

I want you back because I miss you so much

The way you smiled at me and the warmth in your touch

Do you not see the problem or are you just okay with it?

I'm not, and yet you keep hurting me every minute

So I guess this is the end

You no longer want to be my friend

Was this all just a lie?

I gave you a second chance

Played your games and did your dance

Now you want to say good bye

Sometimes I don't believe you

Still thinking that we can make it through

I'm tired of hearing these words

The same hurtful things every day

Things I wish you'd never say

Is this what you think I deserve?

My feelings are not welcome

And you appear to have none

Yet I want you to stay

It's because I'm in love with you

Have faith in us, I will stay true

Just don't push me away

Lightly salted, peppered with problems

I give people too much credit

Hoping that they'll grow up

It's like they don't get it

And most of the time I hate them

I'm not ashamed I said it

I've cut off a lot of friendships

Only sometimes do I regret it

But let it be known

I'm living in a world that's real

While everyone is content being fake

Got me feeling like the third wheel

I'm astounded at their stupidity

The ignorance

The lack of common sense

The whole spiel

I just sit back and sip my tea

Too much lemon in the chamomile

I'm exasperated

Sick of being debated

And tired of being mistaken

For somebody I created in a past life

Reachin' but not grabbin'

Working my ass off but still slackin'

Young in the game but I'm a has-been

Forever stuck in the past tense

Bruises from my schooling

Earn my lumps but I don't choose it

Multiple choices to confuse me

I never fail at losing

It's been a while since we last talked

I know you're mad at me

This has turned out something like I had thought

I wish you had told me how it was going to be

The beginning was happy, everything was good

It all fell into place like I knew it should

But then everything changed and I don't know why

It seems like since then this has been one long good bye

I've changed, I've been worse, I've been better

Things just seem right when we're together

You know all of this and you know what's to come

At this moment I feel really undone

We've been together too long, gone through too much

I can't leave because I would miss your touch

My faith won't run out as long as you're here

I want to be with you, but not live in fear

If it should happen I know my heart will mend

It just won't sit right with me, knowing it's the end

I hope you hear this and understand

Say you love me and take my hand

Be with me always, make this true

God, I wrote this letter for you

That feeling you get when nothing is touching you

But you hurt everywhere

I feel lost, confused and helpless

I don't know what to do

But I have no decision to make

I feel bad

But I haven't done anything

It's a rare feeling

You give me so much
inspiration and fuel
my frustration

Love is a place I am banned from

Yet I see you on the other side

This is hurting my heart

As strong as it tries to be

Your words are like shattered glass

My insides explode

You are so far away

But so close to me

I can't stand the sight of you

But I keep looking

Your song is bittersweet

Why do I do this to myself?

I am just thinking

And you are with someone else

My one true love

Was never mine at all

He never came around

Too busy to call

Just left me hangin'

It's something he does

Now I'm back with this feeling

And memories of what was

So you cried for a week

Well I've been crying for years

Like a Jehova's witness at my door

I'm sick of seeing tears

You must not understand

What it's like to restart

One would think after three times

I would harden my heart

But you've had it all this time

Don't think I'll ever get it back

I bet on you too much

The odds against me are stacked

I've played this game too many times

Thought it was finally over

But this isn't my lucky day

I have no four leaf clover

This feeling, a problem that has consumed me

I just don't know when to quit

Fried brain, broken heart

A recurring, recovering addict

Temporary insanity, that's what I'll claim

Please don't dismiss my case

I'm sorry I can't say things remained the same

But I wiped my fingerprints clean and tried not to leave a trace

This is my first offense

I beg for you to have mercy on me

The time I've done so far has been enough to open my eyes

And I can finally see

This cell I'm held in is already like a prison

And suicide never leaves my mind

I've long since found God

And He helps me through hard times

Somewhere along the way

I ran into the devil

And he's got me doing this hard time

Can I please be released for good behavior?

I hear people in the back whispering, "save her"

No, you just 'gon throw the book at me

Like remember when you threw that book at me?

Still got the scar you slapped on my wrist

I don't want my life to be defined by one crime

But I'm runnin' out of time

When my death penalty is due

Just remember I would have done life for you

Got this pit in my stomach

It's taking over me

I got to confront it

All that's happening

It's nothing I wanted

Trying to build a life

But our growth is stunted

Let it be you and me

But everyone wants in

You open the door for them

It's hard to imagine

You're pulling away from me

Saying you're not

I'm holding on to you

You're all that I got

But me and you together

Is becoming a fleeting thought

You pressed play on a game

I was sure that we forgot

You're forever winning

I'm forever lost

Not on pause anymore

We're completely stopped

You're gonna find out
real soon what it's like to
be too late to make a move

It's so hard to look you in the face

I search for words but they're lost on my tongue

In this relationship, you pick the pace

Beat my heart, expand my lungs

My thoughts are recycled over and over

Our last memory keeps coming back to me

Each visit becomes a date of wonder

I can't help but touch you endlessly

Put my life on pause so I can pray

Cause I don't want God to see me living this way

I've grown up easy

But seen a lot of things

Like that graffiti on the wall

Told me to live like a king

And I'm not gonna lie

Not too sure what that means

I just ask that you show me how to live those dreams

Cause I've been sleeping through life

Only having nightmares

Pretending that I'm not scared

Put on music to calm me

It's playing Maxwell

Cause every time I wake up

I'm hit with morning sickness

(Get it)

I'm struggling in this business

I'm constantly feeling twisted

From dealing with these bitches

And I'm so sorry for cussin'

But something's just not workin'

Been punchin' that clock

Trying to get some time out of it

But it's like it's not up for discussion

So I'm stuck here bustin'

My mind

My ass

Gettin' swept away like trash

Call me a dustbin

Cause I'm tryin' to get it back

Like MJ before he passed

Through all of that

I find myself riding the bike of life

Pushing through the resistance

Needing to get in shape

Cause I can't afford to wait

Spent too much time on things that have gone to waste

And when it gets easier to pedal

I know it's you

Helping me to get done what I need to do

So I'ma press play and get on with my day

Though I've had a lot to say

I know you'll be listening always

I cannot love when someone else has my heart

You want me when you want me

Your words are thrown at me like a dart

Failing to stick so miserably

I hate that you think it works this way

My emotions fall flat when you're true

The tears from my eyes are all that I can say

These words are irrevocably overdue

Saw the rain from a distance

And I waited for it

Like I am for you now

Been waiting for a while

It hits before I'm ready

Loud and threatening

The feeling so heavy

I see it washing away the dirt and the grime

It's amazing what starts to appear

Like going back in time

Or fast forwarding in my mind

Something ancient becoming clear

But the filth from before begins to emerge once more

The rain works harder to make it look like new

What's buried in the earth longs to surface

It's dark and dangerous

And now I don't know what to do

I have no choice but to wait it out

When the rain gets to me like this

I wish for a drought

The virgin is mightier than the whore

Unappreciated

And taken advantage of

I don't care what you say to me

This is not love

Your control-driven nature

Draining me of energy

My tongue has grown tired

Of recapping my history

Trying to change the subject

Make this not about you

Blame me for everything

Even though what you think isn't true

Keep thinking that I don't love you

That I don't care

Strange how in the end

I am always there

One day I will get strong

I won't call

I will not let you know I'm okay

Won't let you know I have been thinking of you at all

I will treat you like you did me

Left me feeling helpless and sad, like I wanted to die

One day I will get the power

To finally say good bye

My eyelashes have drowned in the tears that streak my face

My throat has closed up and disappeared without a trace

Funny how, since you dug my heart out, I seem to feel more

Your evilness finds ways to hurt me, and does so to the core

You don't understand the pain you cause

How you leave me feeling sick

With silence surrounding me

All I can do is sit

I try to think of something else

But my mind always goes back to you

I wish you could see this

Wish you could feel what you put me through

If this is it

I swear, never again will I be this way

You have ruined it for everyone in my life

And not one word to you I will say

I won't think of you, don't want to hear of you

Won't wish you well

You know you are wrong, a terrible person

And for that, you can burn in hell

You took it to heart when I said my feelings were of no concern

We never had a good start, so I guess I gotta do like Usher and let it burn

I play it off like I don't care and put on some Backspin

But I gotta stop kiddin' myself and change it to Toni Braxton

Cause I'll never find the answers to the questions I keep askin'

It's the same routine and I'm tired of the same old thing, but scared of what's gonna happen

See, being with you was never enough, but is it really that rude to want someone so much?

Always startin' arguments and wanting to fuss

I was just trying to switch gears, put your foot on the clutch

Mine was forever down, but you're no longer around

"Unbreak My Heart" playin' on surround sound

And I didn't wanna say anything else that could further hinder myself

But it doesn't really matter now that you've gone stealth

He told me I was amazing

Then let go of the best

I'm trying to get the most out of life

While he's settling for less

My memories of us are fond

I look back on them and smile

But they're starting to get fuzzy

Haven't seen him in a while

I've thought about it too much

Losing its authenticity

And now the truth of what happened

Is becoming a mystery

But that was in the past

And I'm the type to learn from my mistakes

There's always a lesson that's being taught

Hope I can figure it out before it's too late

Kanye said it best

"You worry 'bout the wrong things"

Trying to derail me

Almost lost track of my dreams

Got 20/20 vision

But nothing is as it seems

You told me next

"I should be your everything"

Love, anger, drugs, sex

That's a lot of baggage to bring

You moved me to the other side

Too bad the grass wasn't green

Kendrick is no contest

"The biggest hypocrite of 2015"

Strung out and in a whore

That was the last of you I'd seen

My eyesight is just fine

Cleared a path for me to leave

I'm saying it before the rest

"Cut loose those puppet strings"

I fell hard and became attached

It wasn't easy by any means

But I picked myself up

And now I'm focused on better things

I got excited and decided to finish what I started

Suffering from social syndrome

Throw all my manners out the window

And I would follow them down

While all the lies pass me by

As they crash and burn before my eyes

I keep falling through the surface

Though scared at first, it soon fades

All my feelings go away

Then it suddenly stops

My feet land where they started

The only thought I have is:

"Why should you feel worried?"

After gathering myself

Revelation takes its place

Through a day full of epiphanies

I leave to see what is left

Money makes you lazy

You only good if you you ain't made it

Honest about my work

Never sell myself short

Got a tall order to fill

But sometimes it gets hard to deal

They told me to be myself

But oh, not like that

I'm too dark

I'm too truthful

I'm just tellin' facts

It's hard to pick and choose what words to use

For fear of them being misconstrued

Call it assault with a deadly weapon

Reading these words is killing you

My pen is a bullet

My words speed through these pages before I even say it

I must be constipated

Cause I don't give a shit

Like what you say could ever make me wanna quit

I may as well been doing this since birth

And while I'm here on this earth

The only words that matter about me

Are the ones I write personally

Focus is overrated

The way to get there is lined with the people who never made it

Some say they hate it

Others embrace it

But you'll never see me frustrated

Cause I'm chasing the dream

Only stopping to fuel up my low self-esteem

Getting gassed up on all of the energy you bring

Overstayed my welcome

Guess it's time for me to leave

Hittin' the road

Running on close to no sleep

Completely intoxicated

With the thought of when I can say I made it

Flashing lights behind me from all of my haters

Leaving 'em in the dust

So they can't come bother me later

Seeing my destination up ahead in the distance

Saying a prayer for all of the people who dissed this

Any negativity is automatically dismissed

Never going back to being blinded by ignorance

Mark my words

And have God as my witness

Raining with the sun shining

Can't look at it

Eyes blindin'

Time is an asshole

Days are winding

Don't stop yet

Let me get signed in

Look around the room

Blank faces

Everyday's the same

Familiar places

Knowing I wanna leave

I'm not complacent

Fear's got a hold on me

Hard to face it

Can't let it be the end

I've got determination

So what I have no friends

A living separation

Do it on my own

Remove this hesitation

Get my mind in the zone

Fulfill my inspiration

Thank Jesus

I finally got off that ride

With all the ups and downs

Wasn't sure if I'd survive

Walking away now, wobbly legs

But I hold my head up high

Feeling confident

I conquered it

My fear of it denied

About the Author

Sydney Stapleton is a relatively new author, starting her writing career in 2007. Currently residing in South Carolina with her feline companion, it is evident that she has a passion for writing and storytelling. Her debut book, I Hope This Hurts, delves into the experiences of a young girl who finds solace in writing but struggles with loneliness and misunderstanding.

In the book, the protagonist's inability to connect with others due to her self-doubt and fear of rejection is something that many readers can relate to. The reader will experience the protagonist's hardships from a genuine and real perspective thanks to Stapleton's writing, which will put them in the advocate's position.

www.ingramcontent.com/pod-product-compliance
Lightning Source LLC
Chambersburg PA
CBHW031252120626
46545CB00007B/2768